CH

SPOTLIGHT ON

CIVIC COURAGE

HEROES OF CONSCIENCE™

MALALA YOUSAFZAI

PAKISTANI ACTIVIST FOR FEMALE EDUCATION

Elisa Peters

Rosen
YA™

New York

Published in 2018 by The Rosen Publishing Group, Inc.
29 East 21st Street, New York, NY 10010

Copyright © 2018 by The Rosen Publishing Group, Inc.

First Edition

Library of Congress Cataloging-in-Publication Data

Names: Peters, Elisa, author.
Title: Malala Yousafzai : Pakistani activist for female education / Elisa Peters.
Description: New York, NY : The Rosen Publishing Group, 2018. | Series: Spotlight on civic courage: heroes of conscience | Includes bibliographical references and index. | Audience: Grades 5–10.
Identifiers: LCCN 2017017471| ISBN 9781508177494 (library bound) | ISBN 9781538381229 (pbk.) | ISBN 9781538381236 (6 pack)
Subjects: LCSH: Yousafzai, Malala, 1997-—Juvenile literature. | Women social reformers—Pakistan—Biography—Juvenile literature. | Girls—Education—Pakistan—Juvenile literature. | Girls—Violence against—Pakistan—Juvenile literature. | Pakistan—Social conditions—Juvenile literature. | Taliban—Juvenile literature.
Classification: LCC HQ1745.5.Z75 Y686 2018 | DDC 371.822095491—dc23
LC record available at https://lccn.loc.gov/2017017471

Manufactured in the United States of America

On the cover: This photo of Malala Yousafzai was taken in 2013 in Birmingham, England. The background photo, dating from 2009, shows a girl's school in Pakistan's Swat Valley that received threats from the Taliban.

CONTENTS

FIGHTING FOR EDUCATION

If you've never had to worry about being able to go to school, it's easy to take it for granted—to complain about homework, boring teachers, and annoying fellow students. However, millions of kids around the world don't have the opportunity to get an education and all of the benefits that result from it. Girls, in particular, are often prevented from going to school, or even forbidden.

One of the best-known advocates of education for girls is a young Pakistani woman named Malala Yousafzai. Malala started speaking out in defense of girls' education when she was just eleven, after the Taliban (a fundamentalist Islamic group) seized power in the part of Pakistan where she lived and ordered all girls' schools closed. She refused to be silenced, even after she was shot in 2012. Malala's courage has inspired people around the world. She used her fame for a good cause, setting up the Malala Fund to support girls' education.

Malala Yousafzai is an inspiration to people all around the world. Millions look up to her for her courage, persistence, intelligence, and honesty.

LIFE IN MINGORA

Malala Yousafzai was born on July 12, 1997, in Mingora, the largest city in Pakistan's Swat District. Swat is in northwestern Pakistan. It is the upper valley of the Swat River. The area is known for its gorgeous scenery—dramatic mountains, clear air, lush meadows, and fast-flowing rivers. Its natural beauty made Swat a popular destination for tourists.

Malala's father, Ziauddin, and her mother, Tor Pekai, are from Shangla, a village in the mountains of Swat. They moved to Mingora after they got married. Ziauddin founded the Khushal School in Mingora. He had to work hard and the school made little money in the beginning, but he believed deeply in the importance of education.

Ziauddin also believed in the value of girls. He ignored customs that favored sons over daughters. For example, only males are traditionally listed on family trees in Pakistan. But Ziauddin broke with tradition and included Malala's name.

The Swat Valley is known for its dramatic landscapes. It is home to a diverse mix of plants and animals. The region is also famous for its delicious fruits and beautiful handicrafts.

Her family is very important to Malala (*second from right*). While she is closest to her parents and brothers, she also enjoyed time with her extended family as she was growing up.

Like most people in Swat, Malala's family is Pashtun. The Pashtun people live in Pakistan and Afghanistan. They have a long, proud history and a traditional code of behavior called the Pashtunwali. Malala was named after the Pashtun heroine Malalai, a teenage girl who rallied Afghan troops fighting against the British in the Battle of Maiwand.

Malala spent much of her early childhood playing with neighborhood kids or at her father's school. (Even before she was old enough to be a student, she loved spending time there.) She watched television and played cricket with her younger brothers, Khushal and Atal. They sometimes squabbled, as siblings do. The Yousafzai house was usually full of friends and relatives, and young Malala loved the chatter and busyness.

The family would leave Mingora twice each year to visit relatives in Shangla for the Eid al-Ahda and Eid al-Fitr holidays. Malala loved Shangla and these visits, but seeing the limited opportunities for women in the village made her happy she lived in Mingora.

THE TNSM AND
THE TALIBAN

In 2005, a man named Maulana Fazlullah began broadcasting messages throughout the Swat Valley. Those messages told people that they needed to stop listening to music, dancing, and watching movies. He became known as the Radio Mullah (a mullah is an Islamic religious leader) and was part of Tehrik-e-Nifaz-e-Sharia-e-Mohammadi (TNSM), a group that wanted to impose a radical interpretation of sharia, or Islamic law, on Swat. After a bad earthquake hit Pakistan in 2005, the Radio Mullah claimed it was divine punishment, while the TNSM won support by helping to rebuild villages that had been destroyed.

In 2007, TNSM joined forces with the Pakistani arm of the Taliban, a fundamentalist Islamic group that had ruled neighboring Afghanistan from 1996 until 2001. Even after the Taliban lost power in Afghanistan (thanks to a US-led effort that was a response to the Taliban's support for Al-Qaeda, which had carried out the 9/11 terrorist attacks), they still had local control in some areas.

Maulana Fazlullah, seen here in a still image from a 2008 video, spoke out against many things in his radio broadcast but was especially opposed to women's education.

THE TALIBAN IN SWAT

The Radio Mullah railed against many things he considered un-Islamic, from Western haircuts to vaccinations to women going out in public. One of the things he was most opposed to was schools for girls. Malala and her family worried about the broadcasts, but the Khushal School continued to operate.

In 2007, the Taliban and Fazlullah stepped up their efforts to impose their radical version of sharia. They had first seized power in the mountain areas, but now became a force to be feared in Mingora itself. Supporters broke into people homes to smash up televisions. On the radio, Fazlullah

denounced people who did not support the Taliban. Soon, they even started killing opponents and displaying their bodies in the city's Green Square.

The Pakistani army eventually sent troops to Swat to fight against the Taliban. However, this meant the violence got even worse and the people of Swat had to deal with bombings by both the Taliban and the army.

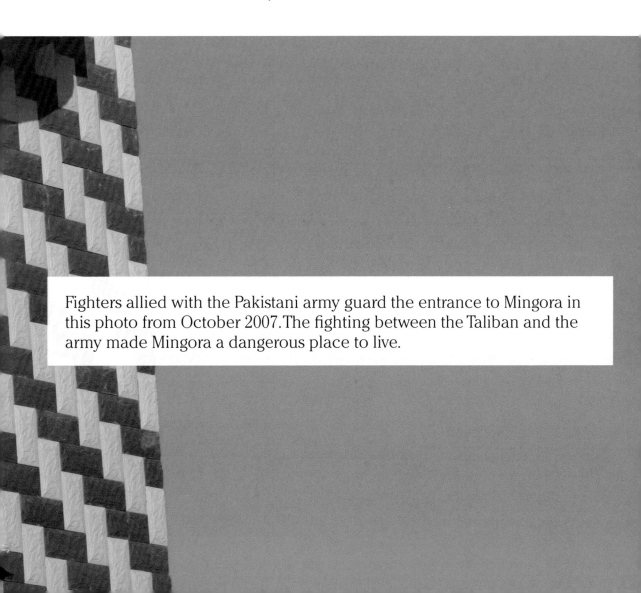

Fighters allied with the Pakistani army guard the entrance to Mingora in this photo from October 2007. The fighting between the Taliban and the army made Mingora a dangerous place to live.

SPEAKING OUT

The fighting between the Taliban and the Pakistani army continued for several years, with the occasional cease-fire. In 2008, the Taliban started bombing schools, especially girls' schools. In December 2008, it announced that all schools for girls must close by January 15, 2009.

A friend who worked for the British Broadcasting Company (BBC) asked Malala's father to find a schoolgirl to write a diary about her experiences for the BBC's Urdu website. They hoped one of the teenagers at the Khushal School could do it, but the girls' families were understandably too scared for their safety. When eleven-year-old Malala volunteered, Ziauddin was proud but worried. They discussed it with Malala's mother, who agreed that it was right to speak out.

On February 3, 2009, Malala's first diary entry was published. The people at the BBC insisted she use a pseudonym so the Taliban would not know whom to target. She picked Gul Makai, which means "cornflower" and is the name of a girl in a folktale.

Malala's fellow students at the Khushal School read and discussed the blog entries she had written for the BBC, but she had to keep the fact that she was the author a secret.

WAR COMES TO MINGORA

Malala continued to write entries for the BBC. They caught the attention of reporters from the *New York Times* who interviewed her for a documentary called *Class Dismissed*. She continued to go to school, but now had to do so in secret. She wore everyday clothes instead of her school uniform.

In April 2009, the Taliban broke their earlier agreement with the government and took over large areas of Swat, including Mingora. That May, the Pakistani Army struck back. Many people, including Malala's family, had to flee their homes. At first, Malala, her mother, and her brothers went to their relatives in Shangla. They later joined her father in Peshawar, a city

southwest of Swat, where he had been meeting with reporters and government officials to try to get help for Swat.

After three months of being refugees, Malala's family finally returned home. Malala was happy to get back to school. She loved learning and was a very competitive student.

The Taliban kept a close eye on how women—such as these high school students from Mingora—dressed, and they cracked down on those who did not fully cover themselves.

A LEADER IN THE MAKING

In 2010, Malala's school took part in the District Child Assembly Swat. Malala was elected speaker of this student government organization. Though she had wanted to be a doctor when she was younger, she had already begun to consider a future as a political leader by this point.

The following year, Malala got the news that Archbishop Desmond Tutu (a human rights activist from South Africa) had nominated her for the Children's Peace Prize, given out by the international group Kids Rights. Later in 2011, she was given Pakistan's first National Peace Prize, an award that would later be renamed in her honor.

Though things seemed to be getting back to normal, the Taliban had not disappeared. By 2011, they seemed to be growing stronger again. More schools were blown up. A few of Malala's father's friends who had spoken out against the Taliban were killed. Then, in 2012, the Taliban put out a death threat against Malala.

Years before he championed Malala, religious leader and human rights activist Desmond Tutu spoke out against apartheid, the unfair system of racial segregation that existed in South Africa from the 1940s through 1991.

A HORRIBLE DAY

The news that the Taliban had called for Malala's death was a shock. While her father hadn't been scared off by threats to his own life, the threats to his daughter's life made him wonder if they should stop speaking out for a while. Malala, however, was determined to continue her advocacy of girls' education. As she wrote, "This was my calling. Some powerful force had come to dwell inside me, something bigger and stronger than me, and it had made me fearless."

On October 9, 2012, two young men stopped the bus in which Malala was riding home from school. It was a beautiful day, and fifteen-year-old Malala was in a

good mood after finishing her Pakistani Studies exam. One of the men asked the driver if it was the Khushal School bus. The other one leaned into the back, where the students were sitting. He asked, "Who is Malala?" Then he shot her.

The shooter who targeted Malala also injured Kainat Riaz (*left*) and Shazia Ramzan (*center*), who were sitting with her on the bus. This photo was taken in 2013, after the girls had recovered from the incident.

SHE SURVIVED!

Malala doesn't remember the shooting. It was her fellow students who eventually explained what had happened. She remembers sitting on the bus; then she remembers waking up in a hospital, surrounded by strangers. She was seeing double and wasn't able to speak because there was a tube down her throat.

Malala had no idea what had happened to her and was worried that her parents would be frantically looking for her. She was frustrated by her inability to communicate. Eventually she learned that she was at Queen Elizabeth Hospital in Birmingham, England. After the shooting she had at first been flown to an Army

hospital in Peshawar. The doctors there removed the bullet and had to also remove a small piece of her skull because of swelling in her brain. She was then moved to a hospital in Rawalpindi, Pakistan, before being flown to England. The doctors weren't sure she would survive, but she did!

Malala's injuries were life-threatening, and the excellent medical care she received from a dedicated team of medical experts saved her life. Here she speaks with nurses from Queen Elizabeth Hospital.

A Long Recovery

Over a week after she woke up in the hospital, Malala's family arrived. She was so overwhelmed and happy to see them that she burst into tears, crying for the first time since the shooting. In early January, she was released from the hospital. The family stayed in Birmingham, and Malala went back to the hospital in February for more surgery. She also got a cochlear implant to help restore her hearing. It took a while for her memory and ability to speak and think clearly to come back. She also had to practice moving her face again.

While she was in the hospital, Malala received get well cards from people around the world. Some were from famous celebrities, while others were from kids like her. She received presents, such as chocolates and teddy bears. Leaders around the world denounced the shooting and there were big protests against it in Pakistan.

This woman holds up a photo of Malala at a protest against the Taliban's assassination attempt on her that was held in Pakistan's capital, Islamabad, on October 13, 2012.

AN INTERNATIONAL FIGURE

Malala was surprised by the outpouring of support for her and determined to keep speaking out once her recovery was well underway. She worked with the British journalist Christina Lamb to write a memoir called *I Am Malala: The Girl Who Stood Up for Education and Was Shot by the Taliban*. She dedicated the book to "All the girls who have faced injustice and been silenced. Together we will be heard." It was published in October 2013.

That same year, the United Nations honored Malala by declaring her sixteenth birthday—July 12, 2013—to be Malala Day. She addressed the UN

Assembly in New York City, calling for education for all children. She explained, "So here I stand, one girl among many. I speak—not for myself, but for all girls and boys. I raise up my voice—not so that I can shout, but so that those without a voice can be heard."

I Am Malala quickly became a best seller. Since its publication in 2013, the book has been translated into forty languages and sold more than one million copies.

THE MALALA FUND

Malala was named one of *Time* magazine's most influential people of the year in 2013. She was also awarded the United Nations Human Rights Prize. Her newfound celebrity meant that leaders around the world were eager to meet with Malala. She met with many, including Queen Elizabeth II of Great Britain and US president Barack Obama. She took the opportunity to criticize the US military's use of drones to carry out attacks in Pakistan.

Malala was also able to use her fame to set up a fund to support girls' education around the world. The Malala Fund was established in 2013 and continues to grow. It aims to make sure that all girls around the world can complete twelve years of quality education. The fund's main goals are to advocate for education, to fund schools and educational programs, and to empower girls and young women to express themselves. It has given away more then eight million dollars.

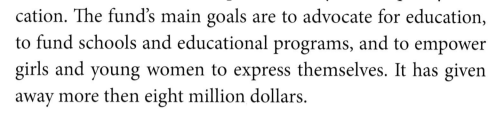

Malala not only won a spot on *Time* magazine's list of the one hundred most influential people in 2013, but she was also on the cover of the issue featuring that list.

The Nobel Prize

Each year the Nobel Committee in Oslo, Norway, gives awards to people who have made major contributions to humanity. Prizes are awarded in fields such as literature, physics, and economics. However the best-known Nobel Prize is probably the Nobel Peace Prize. Receiving it is a great honor. Past winners have included Martin Luther King Jr., Nelson Mandela, Mother Teresa, and the Dalai Lama. In 2014, Malala joined their ranks when she was awarded the prize jointly with Kailash Satyarthi, a children's rights advocate from India. Malala was both the first Pashtun person to be given the award and the youngest person ever to receive it.

In her acceptance speech, she told the committee, "This award is not just for me. It is for those forgotten children who want education. It is for those frightened children who want peace. It is for those voiceless children who want change."

On December 10, 2014, Malala Yousafzai and Kailash Satyarthi accepted their Nobel Peace Prizes together at a ceremony in Oslo, Norway.

Focusing on the World

In 2015, Malala celebrated her eighteenth birthday at the opening of the Malala Yousafzai All-Girls School in Lebanon. The school was set up to provide an education for about two hundred Syrian girls who were living in refugee camps. The girls were refugees because of the long, brutal civil war being fought in Syria. On the same day, the Malala Fund also announced a grant to help pay for girls' schooling at the Azraq refugee camp in Jordan.

Another group of girls that Malala has spoken out in support of is the Nigerian schoolgirls who were kidnapped by the Islamic fundamentalist group Boko Haram. Malala criticized Nigerian president Goodluck Jonathan for not doing more to recover the girls.

A documentary about Malala, called *He Named Me Malala*, opened in the fall of 2015. Malala attended a premiere in New York. While she was there, she once again addressed the United Nations. She also took part in the Global Citizen Festival in Central Park.

Malala attended the premiere of *He Named Me Malala* with her father—the man who had done just that. The movie's director, Davis Guggenheim, has made several well-regarded documentaries.

An Ordinary Teenager

When she is not involved in activism, Malala has tried to be a normal teenager. Though she wants to go back to Pakistan, it is not yet safe for her to do so. Therefore, the Yousafzai family has been making their home in Birmingham. It took Malala and her family a while to get used to living there. Adjusting to a new culture is difficult. Malala began attending high school, but it took her a while to make friends there. English girls interact differently than her friends in Swat had, and being famous didn't help either. In time, she did make friends. She still misses her old friends in Pakistan, though.

Malala's mother began attending a language center, learning to read and write, as well as to speak English. Her father works for the Pakistani consulate and with the United Nations. Some things don't change, though. Malala would still prefer to sleep late in the morning and still quarrels with her brothers!

Malala has spoken about how proud she is of her mother's efforts to educate herself and of how much the whole family has relied on Tor Pekai's quiet strength over the years.

INSPIRATION

Malala has proven an inspiration to many people, but who or what has inspired Malala? Malala's biggest inspiration has been her father. Like Malala, he is a courageous and outspoken advocate for girls' education and for the people of Swat. He is optimistic, probably even more than Malala is.

Although her mother is more traditional, she has supported Malala's independent ways. Malala wrote that, while "My father and I are the starry-eyed ones … My mother is our rock. While out heads are on the sky, her feet are on the ground."

Another figure who inspired Malala is Benazir Bhutto, a politician who served as the prime minister of Pakistan. She was the first female prime minister anywhere in the Islamic world. One of the most precious gifts Malala received while she was recovering in the hospital was two of Bhutto's scarves, which were sent to her by Bhutto's children.

Benazir Bhutto served two terms as Pakistan's prime minister (from 1988–90 and 1993–96). She came from a political family; her father had also been Pakistan's prime minister.

After being named a UN Women Goodwill Ambassador in 2014, actress Emma Watson gave a speech promoting gender equality in which she explained why she is a feminist.

Malala says that a speech by the actress Emma Watson helped her to identify as a feminist. She was also inspired by heroes her father admired, such as Mahatma Gandhi and Muhammad Ali Jinnah, the founder of Pakistan.

There are also people she has met in her advocacy work who inspire Malala. One example is a Syrian girl named Mizune who went from tent to tent in the refugee camp in Za'atari, Jordan, to convince people of the importance of education. In fact, Mizune became known as the "Malala of Za'atari."

Faith has helped sustain Malala and her family through tough times, too. Malala prays regularly to Allah, the name Muslims use for God. She has described how hearing the Muslim chaplain recite prayers and the words of the Quran comforted her when she was in the hospital. Their trust that Allah will protect them helped both Malala and her parents find the courage to speak out.

FIGHTING FOR THE FUTURE

Though Malala is still considering a career in politics to help build a better world, she is focused on her education for the moment. She has taken her A-level exams (exams some British students take at the end of high school), so the next step is university. Her plan is to study philosophy, politics, and economics.

Malala knows she has gotten some criticism in Pakistan. People there are not happy with her popularity in the West and sometimes accuse her of having become too Western. However, Malala still loves Pakistan and misses Swat.

In 2017, she spoke out against the refugee ban put in place in the United States by President Donald Trump. She continues to work with the Malala Fund, which, in 2017, announced the first champions in its Gulmakai Network, an effort to fund locally run education projects.

The fight for girls' education won't be a quick or easy one. But it's impossible to think of a better person to lead it than the smart, brave, and generous Malala Yousafzai.

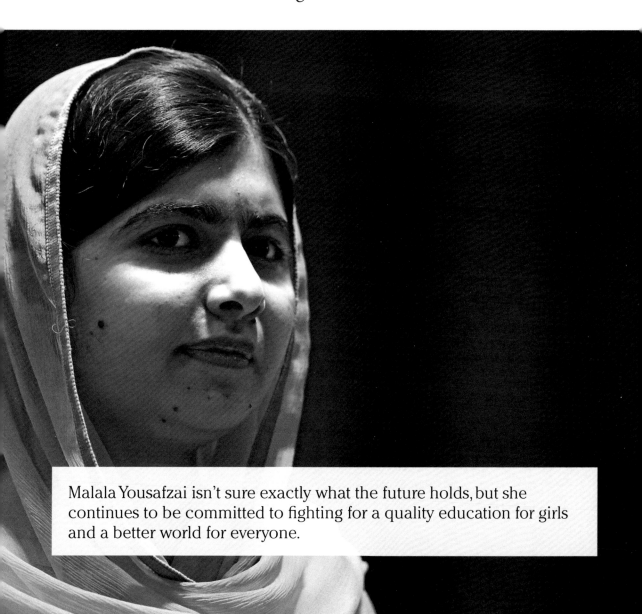

Malala Yousafzai isn't sure exactly what the future holds, but she continues to be committed to fighting for a quality education for girls and a better world for everyone.

GLOSSARY

activist A person who works for a particular cause.

advocate A person who openly supports a cause or action.

chaplain A clergy member who works in a hospital or other organization.

cochlear implant A device placed in the ear of a person who cannot hear to help them do so.

consulate A government office in a foreign country that is there to protect citizens while they are in that foreign country.

cricket A sport that is popular in many parts of the world.

denounce To publicly say that something is bad.

documentary A movie that presents facts instead of an acted-out story.

drone An unmanned aircraft that is controlled with computers.

Eid al-Ahda A Muslim holiday that honors Ibrahim's willingness to sacrifice his son.

Eid al-Fitr A Muslim holiday that marks the end of Ramadan, a period of fasting.

feminist A person who believes women and men are equal and should be treated equally.

fund Money that has been set aside for a particular purpose.

fundamentalist Having a strict, traditionalist understanding of religion.

impose To establish something, or force it on someone.

interpretation An understanding of the meaning of something.

memoir A book that tells the writer's own story.

mullah An Islamic religious leader.

nominate To suggest someone for something, especially for an honor.

premiere An event at which a movie is shown for the first time.

prime minister A term for the head of state in some nations; countries with parliaments tend to have prime ministers.

pseudonym A false name under which a person's work is published.

refugee A person who had to flee their home.

sharia Traditional Islamic law.

vaccination Using medicine called vaccines to prevent diseases.

Equitas – International Centre for Human Rights Education
666 Sherbrooke Street West, Suite 1100
Montréal, QC H3A 1E7
Canada
(514) 954-0382
Website: https://equitas.org
Facebook: @equitas
Twitter: @EquitasIntl
Founded in 1967, the group promotes human rights in Canada and around the world. Its core values are openness, innovation, integrity, fairness, and cooperation.

The Malala Fund
PO Box 53347
Washington, DC 20009
Website: https://www.malala.org
Twitter: @ malalafund
Facebook: @malalafund
Founded by Malala Yousafzai and her father, Ziauddin, in 2013, this organization advocates for girls' education and funds programs and schools for girls. It also encourages girls to learn to speak for themselves.

Swat Relief Initiative
PO Box 860
Pennington, NJ 08534
(609) 474-4987
Email: zebu@swatreliefinitiative.org
Website: http://swatreliefinitiative.org
Facebook: @SwatReliefInitiative
Twitter: @SwatReliefInit
This organization was founded by Zebu Jilani, granddaughter of the last Ruler of Swat. It aims to support health care, education, economic development, and a sustainable environment in the Swat Valley.

The United Nations
760 United Nations Plaza
New York, NY 10017
(212) 963-4475
Website: http://www.un.org/en/index.html
Twitter: @un
Facebook: @unitednations
This international organization was founded after World War II to promote cooperation and peace between countries. Its programs, including the United Nations Educational, Scientific, and Cultural Organization (UNESCO) and the United Nations International Children's Emergency Fund (UNICEF), provide aid around the world

WEBSITES

Because of the changing nature of internet links, Rosen Publishing has developed an online list of websites related to the subject of this book. This site is updated regularly. Please use this link to access this list:

http://www.rosenlinks.com/CIVC/Malala

FOR FURTHER READING

Abouraya, Karen Leggett. *Malala Yousafzai: Warrior with Words*. Great Neck, NY: StarWalk Kids Media, 2015.

Brown, Dinah. *Who Is Malala?* New York, NY: Grosset & Dunlap, 2015.

Frier, Raphaële. *Malala: Activist for Girls' Education*. Watertown, MA: Charlesbridge Publishing, 2017.

Langston-George, Rebecca. *For the Right to Learn: Malala Yousafzai's Story* (Encounter: Narrative Nonfiction Picture Books). North Mankato, MN: Capstone Young Readers, 2015.

Mahoney, Ellen. *Gandhi for Kids: His Life and Ideas, with 21 Activities* (For Kids). Chicago, IL: Chicago Review Press, 2016.

Mason, Helen. *A Refugee's Journey from Syria* (Leaving My Homeland). New York, NY: Crabtree Publishing, 2017.

McAneney, Caitie. *Malala Yousafzai* (Superwomen Role Models). New York, NY: Rosen Publishing, 2017.

Murray, Julie. *Pakistan* (Explore the Countries). Minneapolis, MN: Big Buddy Books, 2014.

Niver, Heather Moore. *Malala Yousafzai: Noble Peace Prize–Winning Champion of Female Education*. Britannica Beginner Bios. New York, NY: Britannica Educational Publishing, 2016.

Stone, Tanya Lee. *Girl Rising: Changing the World One Girl at a Time*. New York, NY: Wendy Lamb Books, 2017.

BIBLIOGRAPHY

Alvarado, Abel. "Syrian Teen Is Called 'the Malala of Za'atari.'" CNN, April 18, 2014. http://www.cnn.com/2014/04/16/world/meast/iyw-malala-of-zaatari/.

Ellick, Adam B., and Irfan Ashraf. *Class Dismissed: Malala's Story*. New York Times, October 9, 2012. https://www.nytimes.com/video/world/asia/100000001835296/class-dismissed.html.

Gidda, Miren. "Malala Yousafzai's New Mission: Can She Still Inspire as an Adult?" *Newsweek*, January 11, 2017. http://www.newsweek.com/2017/01/20/exclusive-malala-yousafzai-interview-davos-540978.html.

The Malala Fund. "What We Do." Retrieved April 2, 2017. https://www.malala.org/about.

Park, Andrea. "Emma Watson Interviews Malala Yousafzai: 'Believe in the Power of Education,' Nobel Peace Prize Winner Says." *People*, November 5, 2015. http://people.com/politics/emma-watson-interviews-malala-yousafzai-on-malala-fund-education/.

Shamsie, Kamila. "Malala Yousafzai: 'It's Hard to Kill. Maybe That's Why His Hand Was Shaking.'" *Guardian*, October 7, 2013. https://www.theguardian.com/world/2013/oct/07/malala-yousafzai-hard-to-kill-taliban.

UN News Centre. "At UN, Malala Yousafzai Rallies Youth to Stand Up for Universal Education." UN News Service, July 20, 2013. http://www.un.org/apps/news/story.asp?NewsID=45395#.WOHu07Sm5FI.

Yousafzai, Malala. "Nobel Lecture." Nobelprize.org, December 10, 2014. https://www.nobelprize.org/nobel_prizes/peace/laureates/2014/yousafzai-lecture_en.html.

Yousafzai, Malala, and Christina Lamb. *I Am Malala: The Girl Who Stood Up for Education and Was Shot by the Taliban*. New York, NY: Little, Brown and Company, 2013.

Yousafzai, Malala, and Patricia McCormick. *I Am Malala: How One Girl Stood Up for Education and Changed the World*. Young Readers Edition. New York, NY: Little, Brown and Company, 2014.

INDEX

About the Author

Elisa Peters grew up in New Jersey and now lives in Long Island. She has had a long-running interest in human rights, education, and the rights of girls. She looked up to Malala Yousafzai before writing this book and does so even more now.

Photo Credits